GW01168264

Small Hadron Divider

DAVID J KELLY

Small Hadron Divider

ISBN 978-1-947271-54-8

text copyright © 2020 David J Kelly
images copyright © 2020 Kate Ramasawmy

Red Moon Press
PO Box 2461
Winchester VA
22604-1661 USA
www.redmoonpress.com

first printing

To absent friends . . .

contents

introduction ... 7

up ... 11

down ... 25

strange ... 39

charm ... 51

top ... 63

bottom ... 75

gluons ... 87

acknowledgments ... 96

introduction

Hadrons are composite particles made up of quarks. The two best-known (and most stable) hadrons are protons and neutrons. Physicists have been fascinated by atomic and sub-atomic structure for the last two centuries — protons were theorised about 200 years ago and neutrons only 100.

Scientists love to take things apart to understand them better, so it wasn't long before they built 'atom smashers', to examine the nuclei of atoms. As the energetic capabilities of particle accelerators increased, it became possible to consider whether protons and neutrons could be 'smashed'. Quarks were discovered in the 1960s.

We now know quarks are elementary particles (i.e. indivisible) and so may be considered the building blocks of matter. They come in six 'flavours', and it is these flavours that serve as headings for the main sections of this collection. It would appear that matter, as well as experience, is far from monochrome. In addition to the quarks, there is a final section entitled gluons. Gluons act, as their name suggests, like glue. They bind quarks together and allow the formation of hadrons. While gluons may well be more interesting than quarks, they receive short shrift here. I'll leave it to experts in quantum chromodynamics to offer more detail.

The most famous particle accelerator is the Large Hadron Collider. I've borrowed from that title for the name of this collection. The word 'divider', was chosen to signify a consideration of the individual flavours, rather than the epicurean car crash that is a knickerbocker glory.

Small Hadron Divider

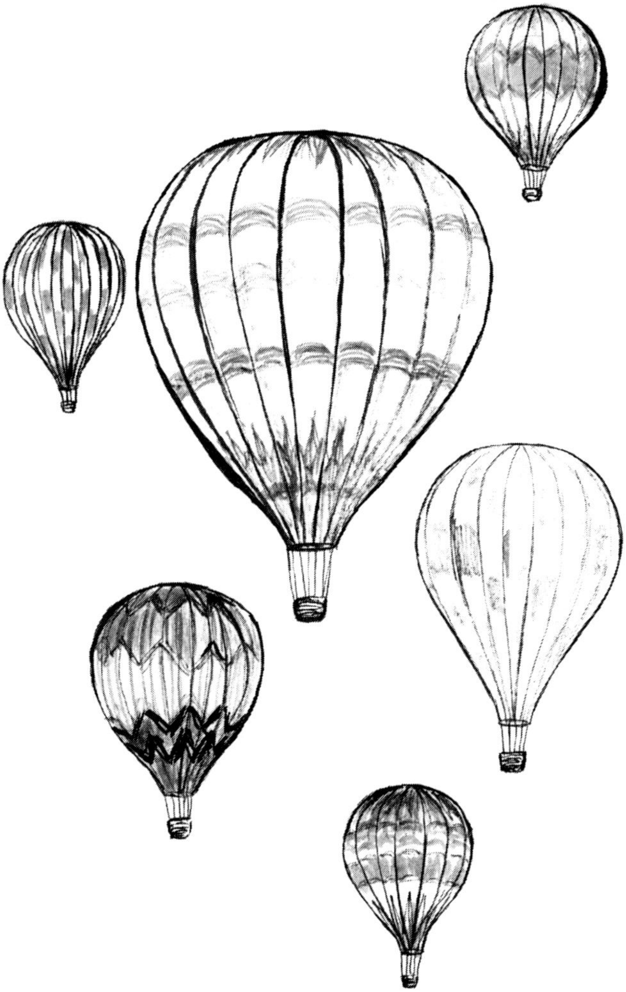

up

Up

I'm no mountain climber; not any more, at least. The routine of office work and the enticing glow of screens draw me to a sitting position too regularly. My weight increases with age, as if the two numbers are in competition. Even so, on rare occasions, I forget my impractical present and tackle a climb. To guard against the humiliation of failure, such ventures are usually conducted under cover of secrecy or anonymity.

>how your praise
>sounds like criticism
>scald-crow

Once I'm out in the open air, memories of former glory return. These are false friends; it never has been as easy as it was. A trick I've relied on, in later years, is to saunter upwards in an almost accidental manner. It's inadvisable to aim at the top; that only invites disappointment. Better to track the transitions in plants and animals, even the landscape and its colours. Then, when something changes, I can reward myself with a moment (or two) to reassess the surroundings.

>slow ascent
>pausing to catch my breath
>the stream runs past

As the years go by, it seems there are fewer and fewer places where you can escape everyone. I try to keep my laboured breathing to a minimum when I meet people. Occasionally their conversations warn of approach, but at other times a gentle "Excuse me" arrives at an inevitably sweaty ear, without warning. After such startlement, my concentration shatters and I watch enviously, as they forge on like helium balloons, inexorably being drawn upwards. I remember, in my youth, I had an attitude to inclines that was quite different. I used to describe it as "falling uphill". Once I'd achieved a critical speed, I could lean into the angle of the slope and it felt like each step was taking itself. That doesn't seem to happen anymore.

> boots off
> a blistered surface
> mountain spring pool

Peaks are chosen with care. If there's plenty of time, the question of success remains "when", rather than "if". Whatever the challenge, it's always sweet to stand at the summit. There's a certain reassurance too, having made it to the natural end of the path and not fallen prey to a medical emergency. Once you're up, the weather doesn't matter. Views might be better in the sunshine, but it's always something special to look down at the world.

> top of the mountain
> every falling raindrop
> assigned a catchment

hawkbit lifting the weight of the afternoon

false dawn birdsong by streetlight

a pale rainbow
stretched across storm clouds
your smile after chemo

needing company
how late the moon
lingers

floodwater . . .
overflowing with questions
schoolchildren

waterboarding
. . . my teabag reappears
at the surface

arising from the sound of water catfishbird

windlass . . .
a girl running
with her kite

double declutching
blown away by a crow
releasing its tree

walled garden
sunlit bricks blossom
into butterflies

first shoots
the rescue party
making it through

spring
swept clean
by its new bloom

crunch of a carrot
standing beside me
the donkey's ears

one foot at a time
learning of the things that lie
beyond the duvet

everyone losing
perspective
guitar solo

arriving late
through the arch
of your eyebrow

dawn chorus this wheat field all ears

Easter Day
the scarecrow's pole
unstaffed

forest fire the whole sky burnt sienna

Early Bird considering the vermicelli

calorie count
from nought to naughtiness
much too quickly

morning after painting over the craic

broken sleep
the wind hurls the morning
around me

deep deep blue
not enough cloud
to hide the emptiness

a small bird's song
the weight of the world
lighter

down

down

trauma counselling
trying to forget
the future

Some people say challenging yourself to do new things helps you grow. Those words seem hollow as my knees struggle to combat the powerful gravity up on the 5m diving platform. I left my comfort zone a couple of flights of steps away, but I'm not sure exactly where. The edge. Despite not wanting to know exactly what five metres looks like, my eyes can't help returning to the edge. I shuffle closer. The world doesn't end. My knees don't buckle. Somehow the drop appears further than it did before. Might be an optical illusion, or the influence of adrenaline. There's a queue forming. I offer up my place to a young lad behind, but he's happy to wait. Okay then, out to the very edge. My mind knows it's water down there, but it looks too solid, like wet glass or concrete. All the sounds are louder. My knees have overcome their battle with gravity and locked solid. Am I stuck? When a hand touches my shoulder, the question is answered.

fight or flight …
I don't want to go back
to the real world

cherry blossom crushed but walking on

downhill
free wheeeeeee
ling

slam dunk a donut lands in my coffee

fallen angel cake
eating it contentedly
a fallen angel

soundlessly
leaves and their shadows drifting
downstream

light and mild
the drinker becomes
the drink

orange-tipped
a butterfly's wing
dips into sunset

an extinct rhino species 49 shades of grey

vermillion too many poppies to count

the fall of civilisation leaf blowers

mourning
broke
n

breaking down
the problem
in pieces

tropical mattress
sharing my bed
with strangers

keepsache

telekinesis
a plasma screen checks out of
the hotel window

behind the pigeon
a folded falcon
unfolding

toffee apple in mid-air and mid-sentence

low income high rise
a wrecking ball swings through
its empty heart

losing the plot
book and reader
slumped on the sofa

kintsugi
the eulogist's voice
between pauses

silence descends
as far as the ear can hear
flake by flake

New Year
in the gentle wind
a leaf turns

brand new jacket
all the raindrops last
a little longer

inside
trying to escape the rain
inside

falling tide . . .
the jumbled kelp grows
an otter's head

strange

uneasy

Too lazy to make an omelette, I tossed the egg into smouldering fat and watched in grim fascination, as the white blistered, then discoloured round its broken yolk. Now, surveying that blind, unblinking eye, squealing like an injured mouse, I can't help wondering if anyone deserves to die alone and in pain.

    doctor's advice
    making plans to stop
    making plans

2wans moving as one
2wans moving as one

haiku journal
the lives of others
breath by breath

the bite mark
without the apple
crescent moon

a ling rook
 rilliant uttercups
a land with no bees

recounting
Goldilocks' history
forebears

parent(s)hese(e)s

cedilla her cough becomes a sough

improved recipe
a new number on
my green pills

b4 d8er inclined 2 1der

r@@@ the postman with some snail mail

no right turn
the voice from the sat nav
falls quiet

hall of mirrors
the multiverse
looking back

Baily's beads an orchard and its black fruit

silly season
unwary spiders
caught on flypaper

overthinking
thinking it over
I'm over thinking

dismembered
but not forgotten
zombie-in-laws

Dali o'clock
a misshapen dandelion
losing its head

clocks go back

recurring dream

no one thinks to change

the pillow cases

sundials

have a new scent

charm

ladybird, ladybird

I used to fly in my dreams. Using a weird arm-swinging action, which I'd perfected in earlier dreams, it was possible to counteract gravity. By jumping into the air and using my clever technique, I could stay aloft. With practice I learned a rudimentary form of steering, but it never worked well in strong winds. On reflection, it was quite like hot-air ballooning, but without either hot air or a balloon.

> frenzied movement
> hides the calm beneath
> inverted swan

Apparently, dreams about flying suggest the dreamer wants to escape from a pressurised situation. That idea never occurred to me at the time. In my dreams, it seemed to me, I was simply showing off. I'd delight in the startlement of passers-by as they met me in mid-flight.

> comings and goings
> between open mouths
> fly-by-night

I've no recollection of emotion from those dreams. The abiding memory is one of curiosity. The ability to investigate a new part of the world and the new perspective it offered. Maybe it was a sort of self-analysis, looking down on my world from a position of detachment. Maybe it was a form of lucid dreaming, where I wanted to fly and found the means to allow myself that indulgence.

> back down to earth
> rising from a pillow
> with windswept hair

raindrops

playing hoop-la

on the koi pond

chick's first meal
the taste of freedom
egg tooth

— — —

the skipping stone's story
unfinished

gentle rebellion
writing in the
reading room

struck dumbilicus

gold's fool
the flash in the
panner's eyes

summer turns to autumn without

mirror bending
beneath the weight of
water striders

a pulse
to every breath of wind
quaking grass

disappearing into heavy traffic a robin's song

call of the wild
in a rural dialect
snaggle-toothed hedgerow

this evening rain
falling into pools
of blackbird song

funeral service a murmuration of memories

baptism of fire
the gingerbread men
meet their baker

country lane
losing myself in the darkness
between stars

autumnal bounty
how little I need
to be happy

seashell —
the roaring emptiness
in my head

misdirection
the importance of being
inearnest

life's too short
the old dog still pulling
at its leash

narcissus flycatcher

Window shopping. Suddenly confronted by my bewildered self. Almost instinctively, I clean my glasses. A pair of unprotected eyes. They draw me in like twin maelstroms. The swirling mixture of summer and autumn adds further confusion. Perhaps these are maps to explain the transition of seasons. The curious palette defies simple description, but they are most definitely not blue. Hurriedly, I conceal them, once again, behind large-framed spectacles and move off, hoping no-one noticed.

> hiding in plain sight
> all the strangers
> on a city street

cOn trails
criss-crOss the morning
tic ... tac ... tOe

spring pasture's sweet scent
a deer's nose not quite touching
the electric fence

high in a tree
playing hide and seek
chick-a-dee-dee-dee

red velvet carelessly unwrapping new antlers

a new skyline
to the hawthorn hedge
hoar frost

mountain tombs what panoramas the dead see

Hogmanay
the skirl of seabirds
from urban cliffs

running water
the river skaters
let it pass

duck dive
fooled once again
by the platypus

up a gum tree do koalas ever know worries?

Sunday best
a fresh wind styles my hair
more casually

flights of geese
the freckled face
of morning

laptop
my cat settles
on the space bar

clean shaven
winter's embrace
more intimate

rebranding
the same head beneath
its new haircut

head space
swinging Schrödinger's cat
between my ears

raindrops
lost in the river
reborn at the cascade

wisdom teeth
learning to chew the fat
without them

forest bathing
lost in an ocean
of thought bubbles

bottom

excremental interest

According to Freud, a child's fascination with bowel and bladder control should be over by the time they are four. That must make me a slow developer, because my interest in poo has lasted considerably longer.

>   milking parlour
>   an old brown cow goes splat
>   against the wall

During childhood my scatological interests extended far beyond the mundane. I was especially fascinated by giraffes chewing the cud. Like cows, they're ruminants, but the food has a great deal further to travel. There's a gruesome magnetism to an animal throwing up a mouthful of partly digested food, munching it for a while and then swallowing it again. Especially when you can watch the bolus shuttling back and forth.

>   rising and falling
>   the level of excitement
>   in a small boy's voice

As a 'grown-up', I've attempted to share this natural wonder with younger generations. Sadly, there isn't always a giraffe handy when you need one. On the bright side, in the pursuit of zoology, I've discovered all sorts of other animals that do interesting stuff with faecal material. Hippos spray it around the place, rhinos trample it in an arena, badgers leave it at their territory boundaries, rabbits eat it for breakfast and dung beetles cut it up into pieces and bury it, like pirate treasure.

>   stool sample . . .
>   it still comes as a surprise
>   being full of it

kcu ʞɔuʞ kcu kcu naw
disembodied tails

low tide . . .
ragged teeth
in the harbour mouth

pearls before time
sediment swirls through
the oyster bed

footloose
a young foal
learning to balance

mixed messages
a child hits the donkey
with its carrot

scratching for a living paydirt

beneath a pine tree
fallen needles
point everywhere

owl pellet . . .
the unpalatable business
of death

dead chameleon
disappearing
into tarmac

Rubik's cubes
getting my head round
wombat poop

half full . . .
telling time by
the whiskey bottle

prayer mat this threadbare hope

self-denial
the best things in life
are not fat-free

river mouth
alternating waves
of salt and sweetness

frozen lava stream . . .
dipping another toe
in the ocean

end of the line
my barren branch
on our family tree

rainy day
children playing
in a pool of happiness

the crackle
of cooling embers
night creeps down the chimney

no rod, no line
the fish watch me
casting shadows

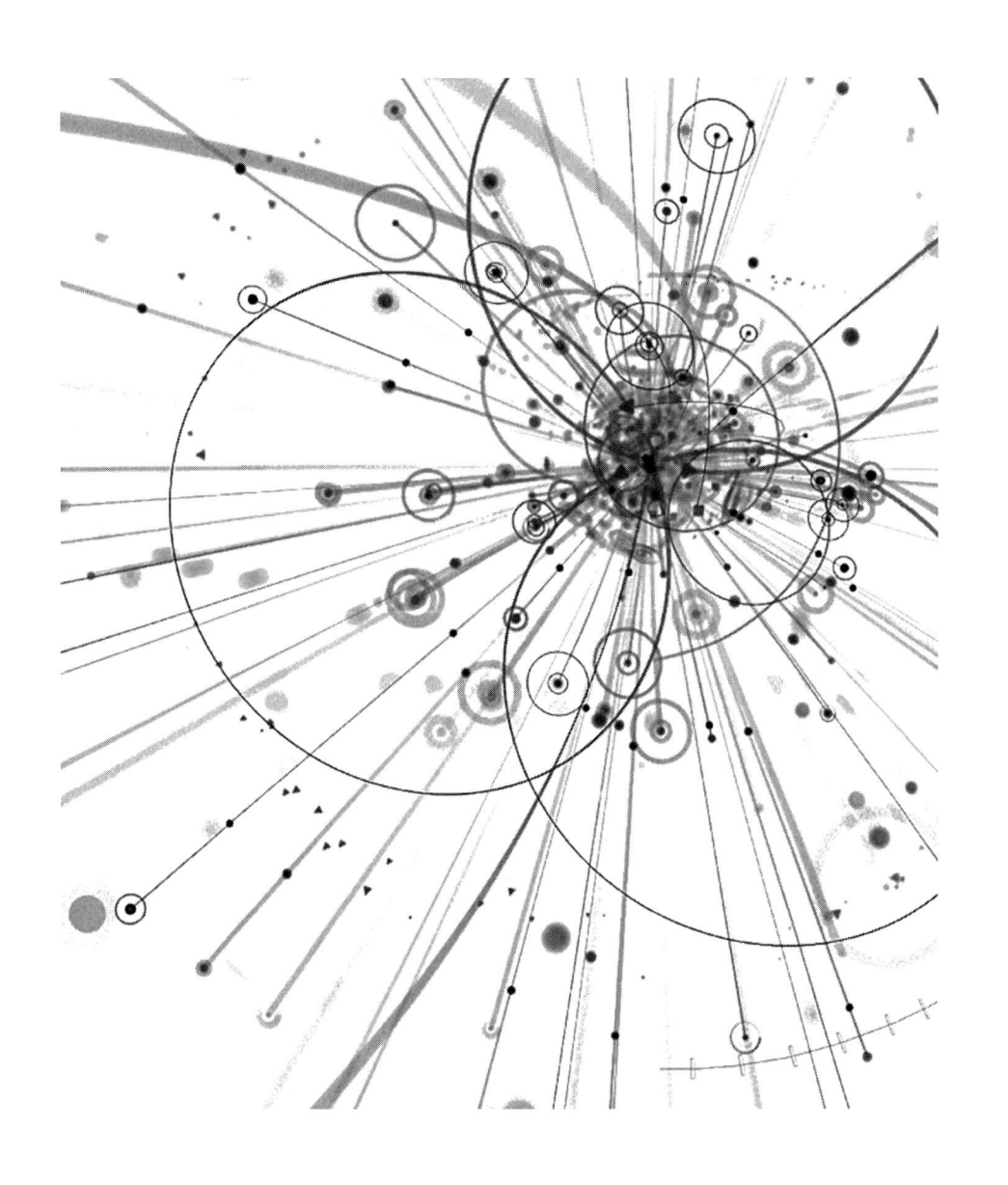

gluons

opposites

Photons of different energies are perceived differently. Lower energy photons appear redder while higher energy photons appear bluer. There are three 'primary' colours; red, green and blue. In combination these give the 'secondary' colours; cyan, magenta and yellow. And if you put them all together, you get white light. So white is all colour information, at once, whereas black is no colour information at all. If an artist were to define black and white, perhaps they'd do it the other way round. A blank page or a starting canvas is often white, but when the artist mixes all colours together in equal quantity, they end up with black. So black is all colour information at once and white is no colour information at all. Is it any wonder that artists and scientists have trouble understanding one another?

> without words
> the lingua franca
> of cherry blossom

hummingbirrd

ecotone
falling leaves meet
rising trout

watched clock
following each second
into eternity

walking between stops bus bus bus

pandemonium
as the huge crocodile snaps
children everywhere

deep in doodle
chasing a thought
across the page

white wash
filling the canvas
with light

red shift . . .
lengthening pauses
in conversation

bullet hole
through a metal door
darkness staring back

a louder silence
the blackbird's pauses
between phrases

a little white lie
the mountain everlasting
losing its petals

end of days
writing on the back cover
of my journal

watched or unwatched
the dying light
slips away

acknowledgments

This collection is comprised of published work from numerous print and online sources. I am grateful to the editors of *Acorn, Akitsu Quarterly, Beechwood Review, Blithe Spirit, Bones, Brass Bell, cattails, Chrysanthemum, Contemporary Haibun Online, Creatrix, Echidna Tracks, ephemerae, Failed Haiku, Frogpond, Ginyu, Grievous Angel, Haibun Today, Haiku Canada Review, Hedgerow, Kokako, Mariposa, Modern Haiku, moongarlic, Otata, Presence, Prune Juice, seashores, Shamrock, Star*Line, Stone after Stone* anthology, *The Bamboo Hut, The Cicada's Cry, The Haibun Journal, The Heron's Nest, The Mamba, Time Haiku, tinywords, Under the Basho, undertow, vines* and *Wales Haiku Journal* for including my work in their journals.

This collection contains more haibun than its predecessor. That is, in no small part, due to the feedback, discussions, guidance and encouragement I have had from the members of the Pepperpots Haibun Group. My thanks to you all.

Finally, I hope you will enjoy the beautiful illustrations on the cover and at each section heading. These are the work of the very talented Kate Ramasawmy. My thanks to her for venturing into uncharted territory with a new collaborator.